TupperKids™

Christmas

Fun for

KIDS

Stories, Crafts, Songs, and More

This publication is brought to you through the joint efforts of
Tupperware U.S., Inc., and Publications International, Ltd.

Contributing Illustrators: Susan Spellman, Jerry Tiritilli,
Kathleen O'Malley, Linda Graves, Tim Ellis

Contributing Writers: Carolyn Quattrocki, Jane Jerrard

Contributing Craft Designer and Craft Illustration:
Cindy Groom Harry® and Staff, Designs & Consultation

Contributing Crafter: Bev George

Photography by Sacco Productions Limited/Chicago

Photographers: Tom O'Connell, Rick Tragesser

Photo Stylist: Melissa Frisco

Photo Production: Paula M. Walters

Food Stylists: Donna Coates, Teri Rys–Maki

Assistant Food Stylists: Kim Hartman, Laura Hess

"'Twas the Night Before Christmas" was written by Clement Moore.

Louis Weber, C.E.O.
Publications International, Ltd.
7373 North Cicero Avenue
Lincolnwood, Illinois 60646

Permission is never granted for commercial purposes.

Manufactured in U.S.A.

8 7 6 5 4 3 2 1

ISBN: 0–7853–1036–3

CONTENTS

'TWAS THE NIGHT BEFORE
CHRISTMAS

'Twas the night before Christmas,
    when all through the house
Not a creature was stirring,
    not even a mouse.
The stockings were hung
    by the chimney with care,
In hopes that Saint Nicholas
    soon would be there.
The children were nestled
    all snug in their beds,
While visions of sugarplums
    danced in their heads;

And mamma in her kerchief,
    and I in my cap,
Had just settled our brains
    for a long winter's nap—
When out on the lawn
    there arose such a clatter
I sprang from my bed
    to see what was the matter.
Away to the window
    I flew like a flash,
Tore open the shutter,
    and threw up the sash.

The moon on the breast
of the new-fallen snow
Gave a luster of midday
to objects below;
When what to my
wondering eyes should appear
But a miniature sleigh
and eight tiny reindeer,
With a little old driver,
so lively and quick,
I knew in a moment
it must be Saint Nick!

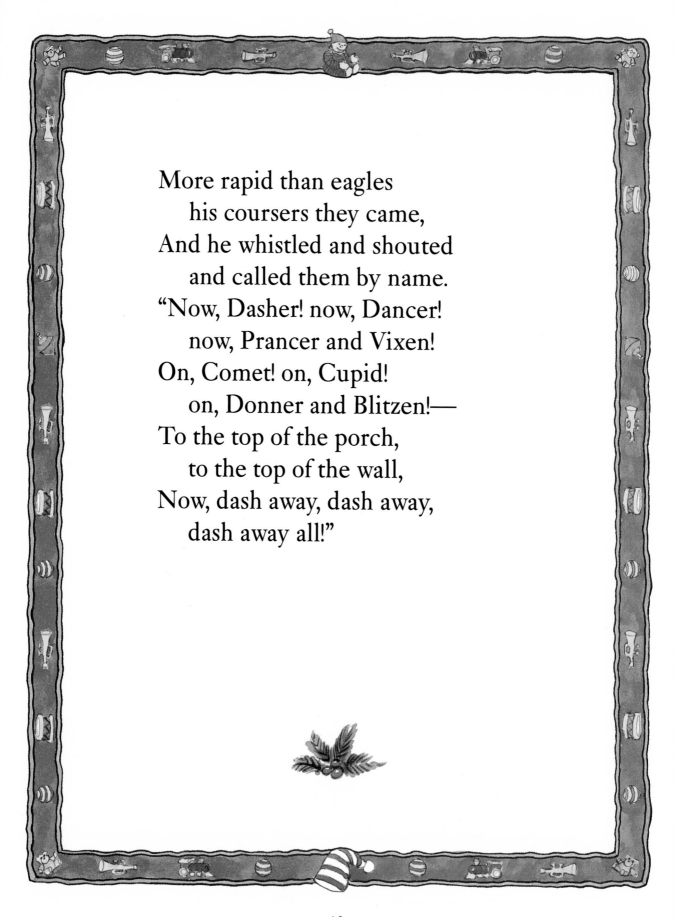

More rapid than eagles
   his coursers they came,
And he whistled and shouted
   and called them by name.
"Now, Dasher! now, Dancer!
   now, Prancer and Vixen!
On, Comet! on, Cupid!
   on, Donner and Blitzen!—
To the top of the porch,
   to the top of the wall,
Now, dash away, dash away,
   dash away all!"

As dry leaves that before
the wild hurricane fly,
When they meet with an obstacle
mount to the sky,
So, up to the housetop
the coursers they flew,
With a sleigh full of toys—
and Saint Nicholas, too.
And then, in a twinkling,
I heard on the roof,
The prancing and pawing
of each little hoof.

13

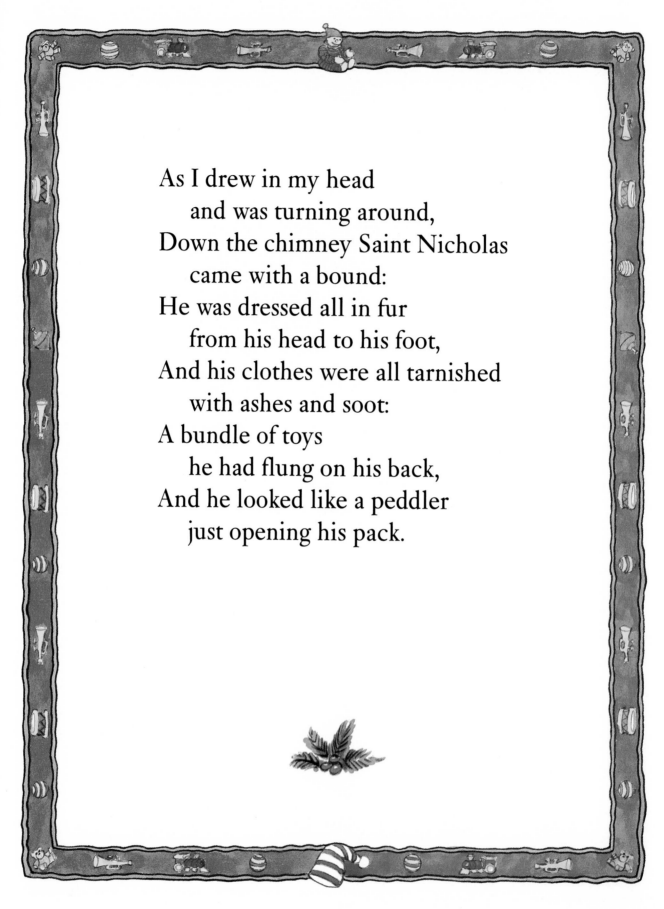

As I drew in my head
    and was turning around,
Down the chimney Saint Nicholas
    came with a bound:
He was dressed all in fur
    from his head to his foot,
And his clothes were all tarnished
    with ashes and soot:
A bundle of toys
    he had flung on his back,
And he looked like a peddler
    just opening his pack.

His eyes, how they twinkled!
    his dimples, how merry!
His cheeks were like roses,
    his nose like a cherry;
His droll little mouth
    was drawn up like a bow,
And the beard on his chin
    was as white as the snow.

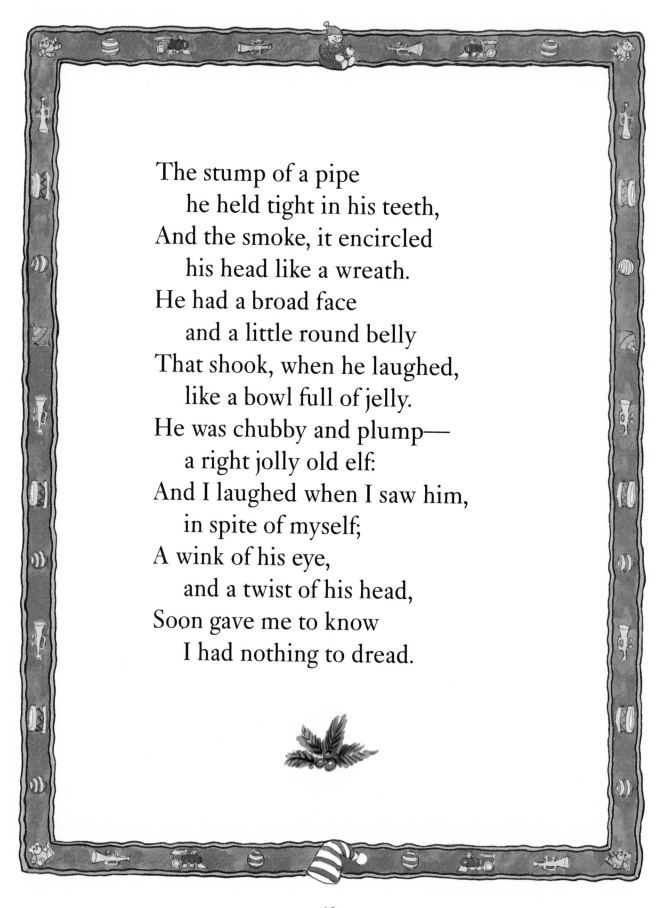

The stump of a pipe
    he held tight in his teeth,
And the smoke, it encircled
    his head like a wreath.
He had a broad face
    and a little round belly
That shook, when he laughed,
    like a bowl full of jelly.
He was chubby and plump—
    a right jolly old elf:
And I laughed when I saw him,
    in spite of myself;
A wink of his eye,
    and a twist of his head,
Soon gave me to know
    I had nothing to dread.

19

He spoke not a word,
   but went straight to his work,
And filled all the stockings:
   then turned with a jerk,
And laying a finger
   aside of his nose,
 And giving a nod,
   up the chimney he rose.
He sprang to his sleigh,
   to his team gave a whistle,
 And away they all flew
   like the down of a thistle.
But I heard him exclaim,
   ere they drove out of sight,
"Happy Christmas to all,
   and to all a good-night!"

On the night before Christmas,
  Santa's elves are so busy,
Just watching them rush
  could make you dizzy!
They trip over each other,
  and stumble over themselves—
It's hard to say which
  is the clumsiest elf!

The elves are in such a hurry,
some of the presents aren't
coming out quite right. Can you
find Santa? Can you find these
unusual presents?

An airplane

Roller skates

A tea set

A clock

A stuffed animal

A football

A doll

A hockey stick

A bicycle

'Twas the night before Christmas,
   when all are asleep.
They're snug in their beds
   and they're counting their sheep.
Santa shouts as his sleigh
   disappears out of sight,
"Merry Christmas to all,
   and to all a good night!"

It's getting late, and everyone is still
stirring! Can you find Santa and his
eight reindeer? Then find these
bedtime things.

A bedtime story

A Rudolph nightlight

A nightgown

A nightcap

A pair of fuzzy slippers

A teddy bear

A toothbrush

Six sheep for the children to count

Santa Claus Stocking

MATERIALS
Felt: two 9 x 12 inches white, 3 x 4
 inches beige, 5 x 5 inches red, and
 1 x 1 inch red
Red satin ribbon: 1-yard 3-inch length
 of ⅝-inch wide, 11-inch
 length of ⅛-inch wide
Small amount fiberfill
Poms: 1-inch white, ¼-inch red
White jumbo loopy chenille, 8-inch
 length
Two wiggle eyes, 10mm each
White chenille stem, 1½-inch length
Thick white craft glue
Glue gun (set on low temperature)
Scissors
Ruler

1. Using the patterns to make the front of the stocking, trace and cut the stocking foot and cuff from the white felt. Apply craft glue to the top edge of the stocking. Overlap the top edge of the stocking with the bottom edge of the cuff about ¼ inch. Allow the glue to dry.

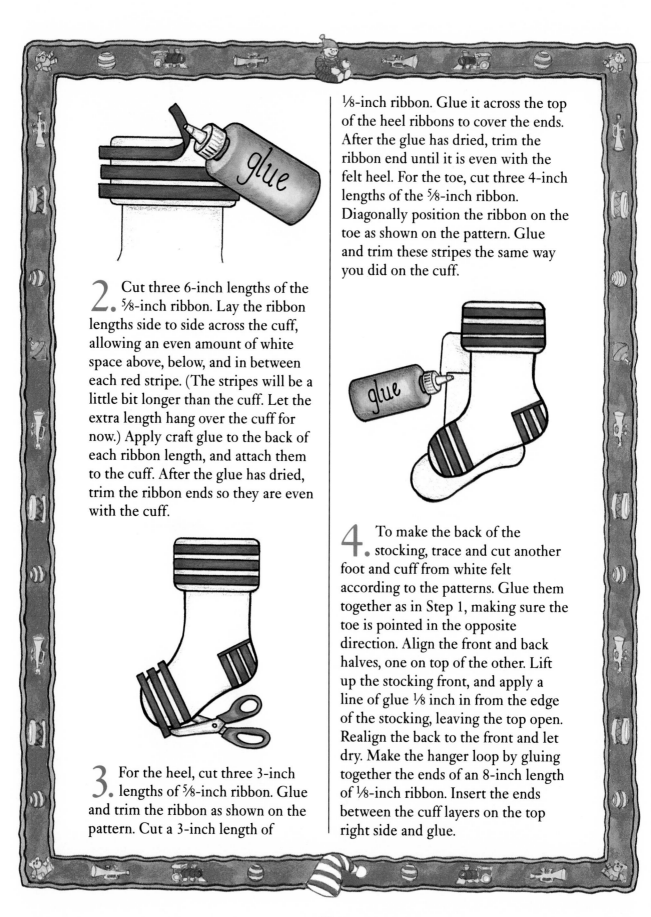

2. Cut three 6-inch lengths of the ⅝-inch ribbon. Lay the ribbon lengths side to side across the cuff, allowing an even amount of white space above, below, and in between each red stripe. (The stripes will be a little bit longer than the cuff. Let the extra length hang over the cuff for now.) Apply craft glue to the back of each ribbon length, and attach them to the cuff. After the glue has dried, trim the ribbon ends so they are even with the cuff.

3. For the heel, cut three 3-inch lengths of ⅝-inch ribbon. Glue and trim the ribbon as shown on the pattern. Cut a 3-inch length of ⅛-inch ribbon. Glue it across the top of the heel ribbons to cover the ends. After the glue has dried, trim the ribbon end until it is even with the felt heel. For the toe, cut three 4-inch lengths of the ⅝-inch ribbon. Diagonally position the ribbon on the toe as shown on the pattern. Glue and trim these stripes the same way you did on the cuff.

4. To make the back of the stocking, trace and cut another foot and cuff from white felt according to the patterns. Glue them together as in Step 1, making sure the toe is pointed in the opposite direction. Align the front and back halves, one on top of the other. Lift up the stocking front, and apply a line of glue ⅛ inch in from the edge of the stocking, leaving the top open. Realign the back to the front and let dry. Make the hanger loop by gluing together the ends of an 8-inch length of ⅛-inch ribbon. Insert the ends between the cuff layers on the top right side and glue.

6. For the beard, bend the jumbo loopy chenille into a "C" shape and glue around the face. Glue the red pom nose and wiggle eyes to the center of the face. Glue the mouth and then the mustache onto the face below the nose. For the eyebrows, cut two ¾-inch lengths of chenille stem and bend each to curve. Glue above the eyes.

5. Using the patterns to make Santa, trace and cut the face from the beige felt, the hat and the mouth from the red felt, and the mustache from the white felt. To assemble, use the glue gun. For the hat, roll the red felt into a cone shape, slightly overlapping the straight sides. Glue the overlap area together. Position and glue the top of the face inside the hat. Glue the face and the lower back of the hat to the stocking. Apply glue to the lower edge of the hat and attach fiberfill. Fold over the tip of the hat and glue to the stocking. Glue a white pom on the tip of the hat.

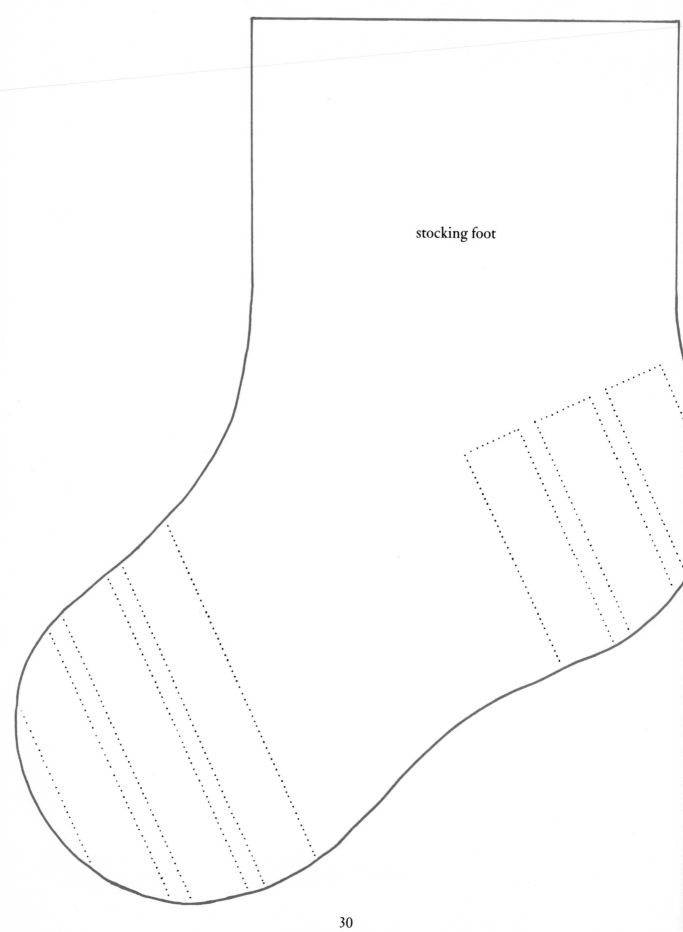

stocking foot

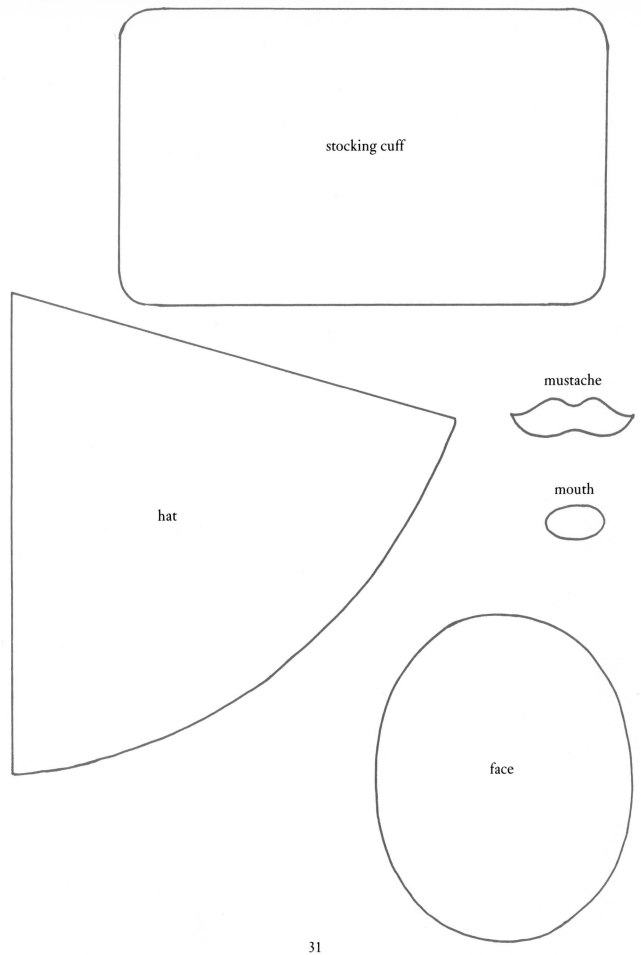

stocking cuff

mustache

mouth

hat

face

THE HAPPY SNOWMAN

"It's snowing! Come look, Matt," cried Jenny. "It's coming down so fast I can hardly see across the street!" Matt ran to the window. Jenny was right! The snow was covering everything in sight. He could hardly wait to go outside to play in the snow! He was sure all their friends would be at the park.

Matt and Jenny ran to find their snow boots. "I want to come, too!" said Marianna. She always wanted to go wherever they went. "No," said Matt. "You're too little to go to the park with us now. Maybe later."

Jenny and Matt hurried to put on hats, mittens, and scarves. They called goodbye to their mother and raced out the door.

Lisa, Tracy, and Paul were already at the park by the time Matt and Jenny got there. "Isn't this the greatest?" said Tracy. "The snow's so deep!" "Let's build a snowman," said Paul. "A huge snowman—as tall as we can make him."

They got to work. It wasn't easy. They had to roll one great big snowball for his body, another for his chest, and then a smaller one for his head. Then Jenny said, "He needs a face and some clothes." Everyone ran home to see what they could find.

Lisa found some bright, black pieces of coal for his eyes and a button for his nose. Tracy borrowed her big brother's purple scarf, and Paul brought the toy corncob pipe from his Halloween costume.

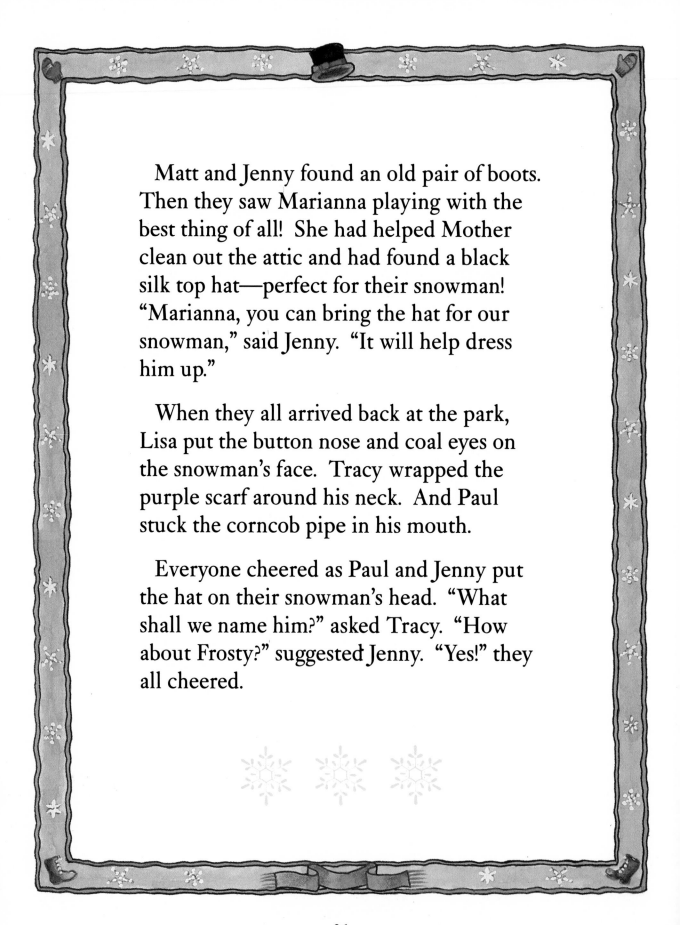

Matt and Jenny found an old pair of boots. Then they saw Marianna playing with the best thing of all! She had helped Mother clean out the attic and had found a black silk top hat—perfect for their snowman! "Marianna, you can bring the hat for our snowman," said Jenny. "It will help dress him up."

When they all arrived back at the park, Lisa put the button nose and coal eyes on the snowman's face. Tracy wrapped the purple scarf around his neck. And Paul stuck the corncob pipe in his mouth.

Everyone cheered as Paul and Jenny put the hat on their snowman's head. "What shall we name him?" asked Tracy. "How about Frosty?" suggested Jenny. "Yes!" they all cheered.

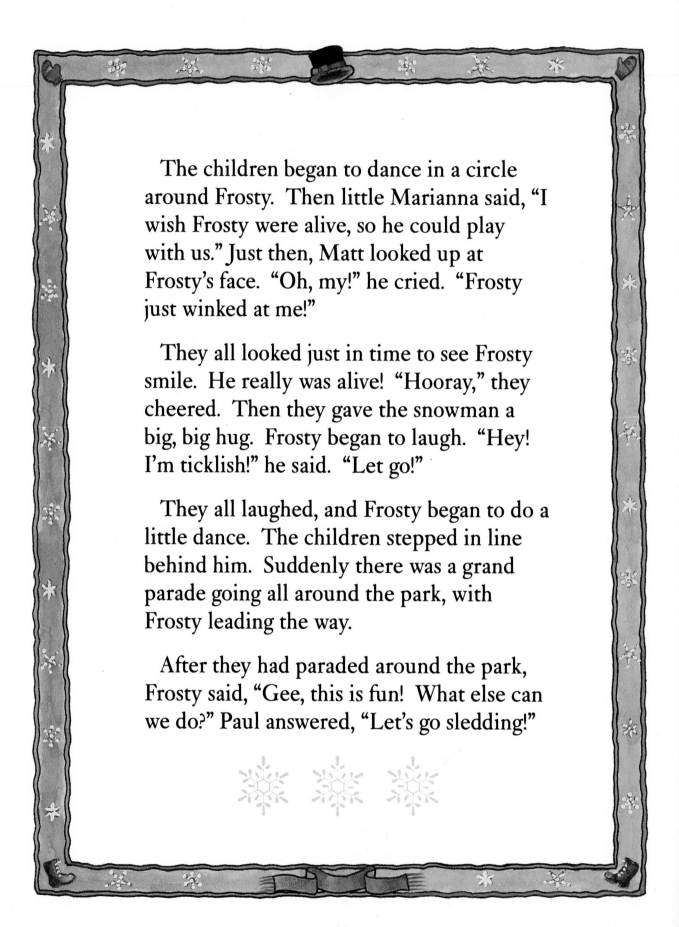

The children began to dance in a circle around Frosty. Then little Marianna said, "I wish Frosty were alive, so he could play with us." Just then, Matt looked up at Frosty's face. "Oh, my!" he cried. "Frosty just winked at me!"

They all looked just in time to see Frosty smile. He really was alive! "Hooray," they cheered. Then they gave the snowman a big, big hug. Frosty began to laugh. "Hey! I'm ticklish!" he said. "Let go!"

They all laughed, and Frosty began to do a little dance. The children stepped in line behind him. Suddenly there was a grand parade going all around the park, with Frosty leading the way.

After they had paraded around the park, Frosty said, "Gee, this is fun! What else can we do?" Paul answered, "Let's go sledding!"

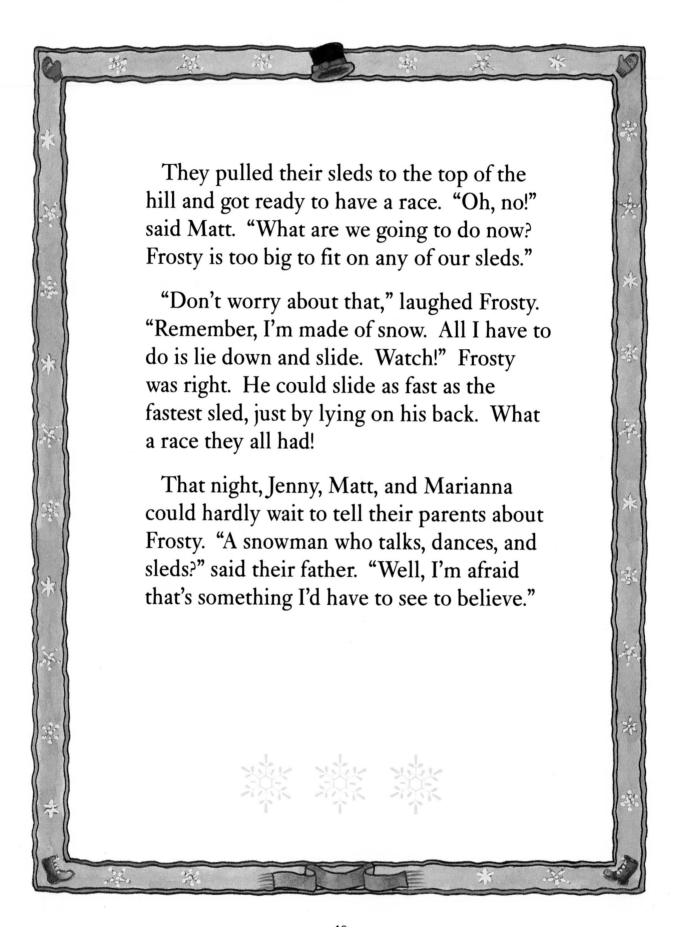

They pulled their sleds to the top of the hill and got ready to have a race. "Oh, no!" said Matt. "What are we going to do now? Frosty is too big to fit on any of our sleds."

"Don't worry about that," laughed Frosty. "Remember, I'm made of snow. All I have to do is lie down and slide. Watch!" Frosty was right. He could slide as fast as the fastest sled, just by lying on his back. What a race they all had!

That night, Jenny, Matt, and Marianna could hardly wait to tell their parents about Frosty. "A snowman who talks, dances, and sleds?" said their father. "Well, I'm afraid that's something I'd have to see to believe."

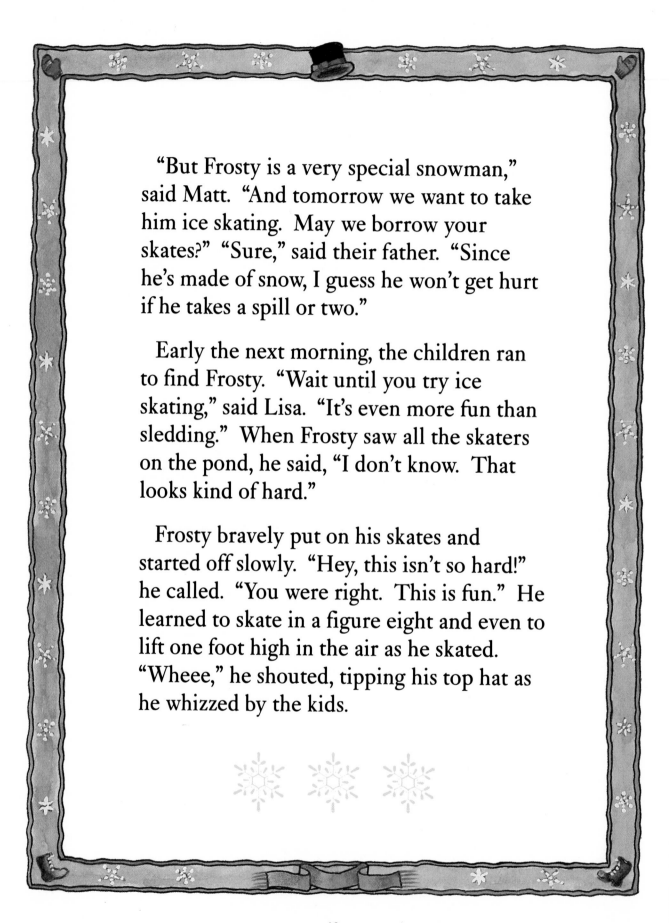

"But Frosty is a very special snowman," said Matt. "And tomorrow we want to take him ice skating. May we borrow your skates?" "Sure," said their father. "Since he's made of snow, I guess he won't get hurt if he takes a spill or two."

Early the next morning, the children ran to find Frosty. "Wait until you try ice skating," said Lisa. "It's even more fun than sledding." When Frosty saw all the skaters on the pond, he said, "I don't know. That looks kind of hard."

Frosty bravely put on his skates and started off slowly. "Hey, this isn't so hard!" he called. "You were right. This is fun." He learned to skate in a figure eight and even to lift one foot high in the air as he skated. "Wheee," he shouted, tipping his top hat as he whizzed by the kids.

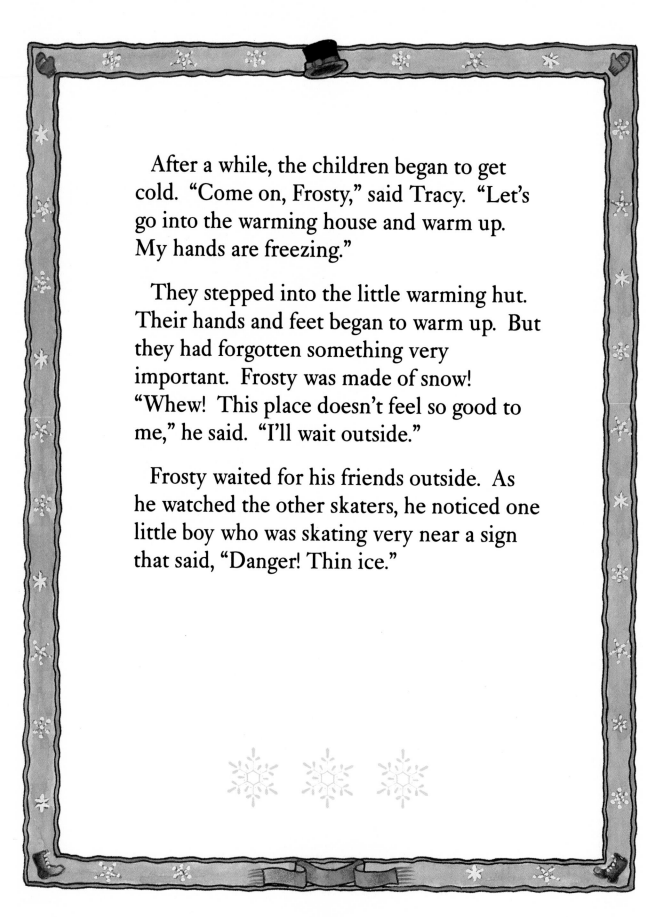

After a while, the children began to get
cold. "Come on, Frosty," said Tracy. "Let's
go into the warming house and warm up.
My hands are freezing."

They stepped into the little warming hut.
Their hands and feet began to warm up. But
they had forgotten something very
important. Frosty was made of snow!
"Whew! This place doesn't feel so good to
me," he said. "I'll wait outside."

Frosty waited for his friends outside. As
he watched the other skaters, he noticed one
little boy who was skating very near a sign
that said, "Danger! Thin ice."

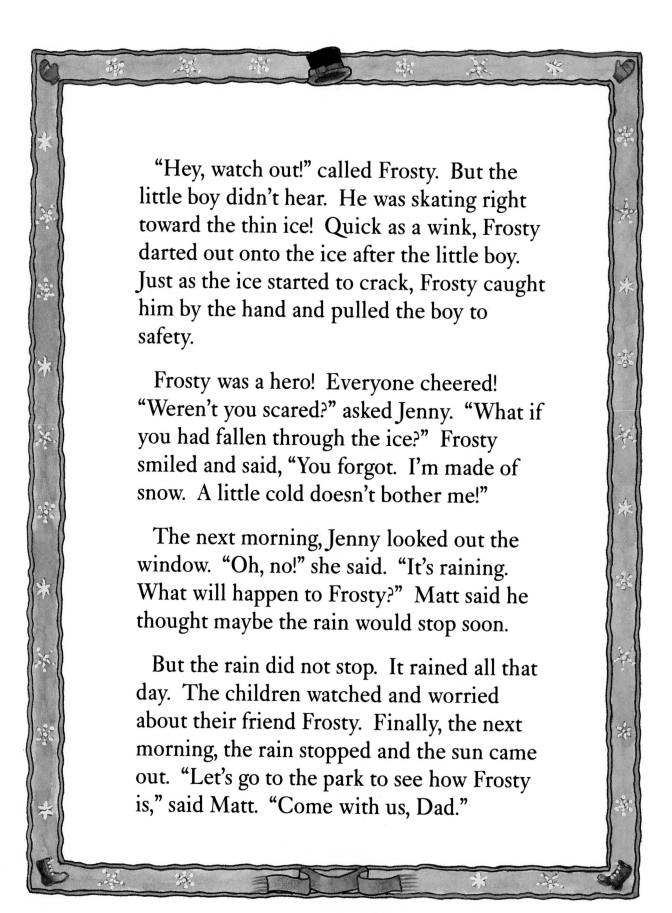

"Hey, watch out!" called Frosty. But the little boy didn't hear. He was skating right toward the thin ice! Quick as a wink, Frosty darted out onto the ice after the little boy. Just as the ice started to crack, Frosty caught him by the hand and pulled the boy to safety.

Frosty was a hero! Everyone cheered! "Weren't you scared?" asked Jenny. "What if you had fallen through the ice?" Frosty smiled and said, "You forgot. I'm made of snow. A little cold doesn't bother me!"

The next morning, Jenny looked out the window. "Oh, no!" she said. "It's raining. What will happen to Frosty?" Matt said he thought maybe the rain would stop soon.

But the rain did not stop. It rained all that day. The children watched and worried about their friend Frosty. Finally, the next morning, the rain stopped and the sun came out. "Let's go to the park to see how Frosty is," said Matt. "Come with us, Dad."

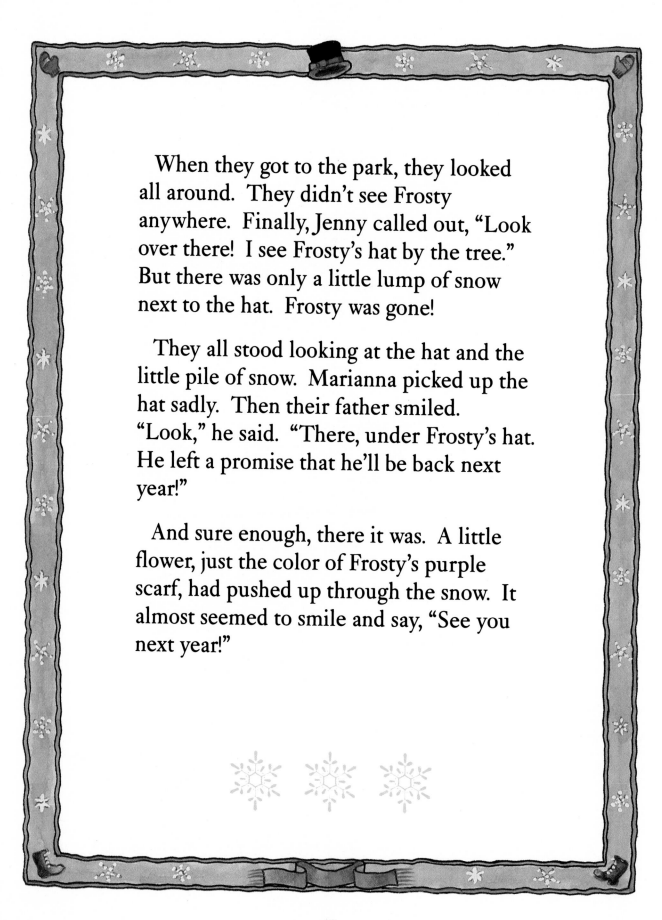

When they got to the park, they looked all around. They didn't see Frosty anywhere. Finally, Jenny called out, "Look over there! I see Frosty's hat by the tree." But there was only a little lump of snow next to the hat. Frosty was gone!

They all stood looking at the hat and the little pile of snow. Marianna picked up the hat sadly. Then their father smiled. "Look," he said. "There, under Frosty's hat. He left a promise that he'll be back next year!"

And sure enough, there it was. A little flower, just the color of Frosty's purple scarf, had pushed up through the snow. It almost seemed to smile and say, "See you next year!"

Frosty, the Snowman
Was a jolly, happy soul!

Hey! This song is about me! I made a lot of friends the day the children put a magic top hat on my head and a broomstick in my hand. Boy, were they surprised when I began to sing and dance!

Can you find me? Can you find my friends who chased me all around, playing catch-me-if-you-can?

Kevin

Mark

Lee

Michael

Claire

Scotty

Jenny

O Christmas tree,
O Christmas tree,
How lovely are your branches!

Boy, it's sure getting close to Christmas! Here's a little town that means business when it's time to decorate Christmas trees!

Can you find my favorite ornaments? I'll give you a hint: The trees match a store. After you've admired the decorations, see if you can find me!

Dog bone

Pink ornament

Slice of pie

Panda bear

High-heeled shoe

Button

Music note

Lollipop

Wrench

ONE-HOUR

Snowman Sweatshirt

MATERIALS

Dimensional paint: black, glittering
   crystal

Red sweatshirt

Felt: 8 x 10 inches white, 2 x 4 inches
   black, 1 x 3 inches red, 1 x 2 inches
   pink

Two green poms, ¾ inch each

Two wiggle eyes, 10mm each

Four black half-ball buttons, ⁵⁄₁₆ inch
   each

2-inch yellow feather

Red/green plaid ribbon, 14-inch
   length of ⁵⁄₈-inch wide

Glue gun (set on low temperature)

Scissors

Ruler

Craft snips

Paintbrush

Repositionable glue

1. Randomly squeeze-paint glittering crystal snowflakes on the shirt front by painting a cross out of a 1-inch horizontal line and a 1-inch vertical line. Then paint two ¾-inch diagonal lines forming an X on top of the cross. Let paint dry. Repeat on shirt back.

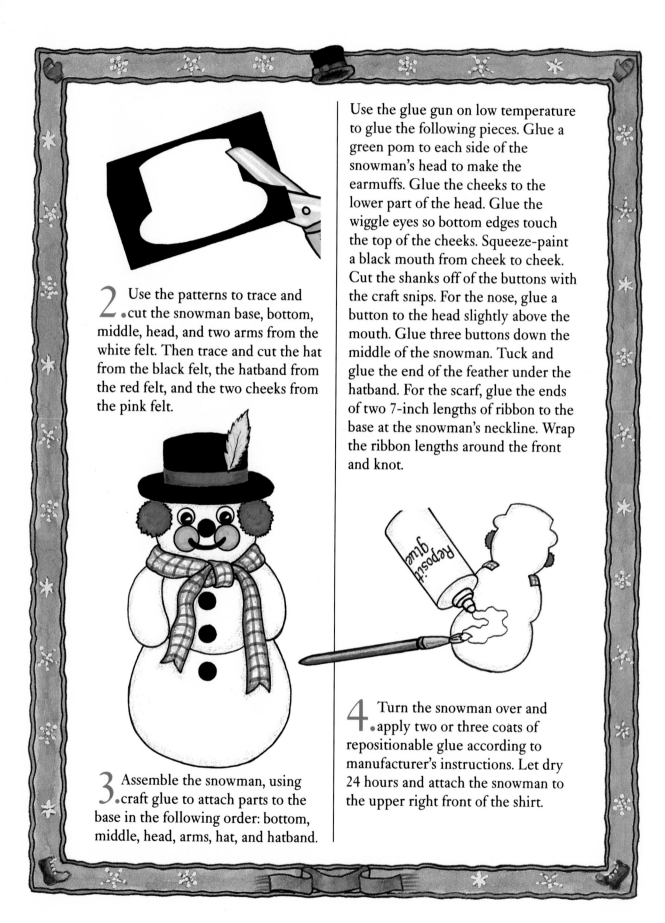

2. Use the patterns to trace and cut the snowman base, bottom, middle, head, and two arms from the white felt. Then trace and cut the hat from the black felt, the hatband from the red felt, and the two cheeks from the pink felt.

Use the glue gun on low temperature to glue the following pieces. Glue a green pom to each side of the snowman's head to make the earmuffs. Glue the cheeks to the lower part of the head. Glue the wiggle eyes so bottom edges touch the top of the cheeks. Squeeze-paint a black mouth from cheek to cheek. Cut the shanks off of the buttons with the craft snips. For the nose, glue a button to the head slightly above the mouth. Glue three buttons down the middle of the snowman. Tuck and glue the end of the feather under the hatband. For the scarf, glue the ends of two 7-inch lengths of ribbon to the base at the snowman's neckline. Wrap the ribbon lengths around the front and knot.

3. Assemble the snowman, using craft glue to attach parts to the base in the following order: bottom, middle, head, arms, hat, and hatband.

4. Turn the snowman over and apply two or three coats of repositionable glue according to manufacturer's instructions. Let dry 24 hours and attach the snowman to the upper right front of the shirt.

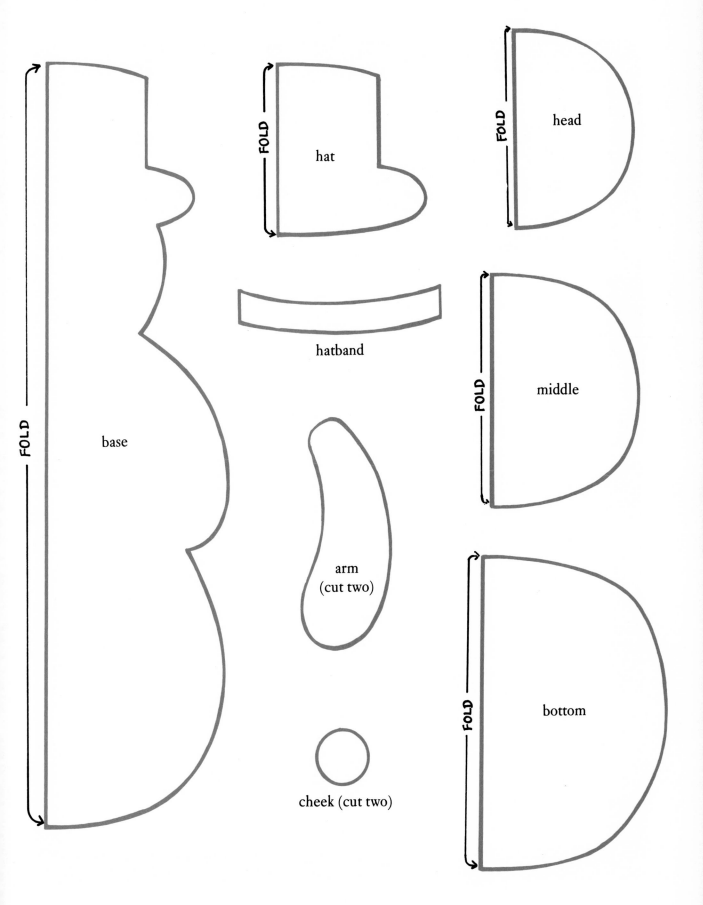

base

FOLD

hat

FOLD

head

FOLD

hatband

middle

FOLD

arm
(cut two)

bottom

FOLD

cheek (cut two)

RUDOLPH'S
ADVENTURE

It's Christmas Eve in Reindeer Land! All the little reindeer are excited because Santa Claus will visit this very night. A blanket of new snow has fallen on the ground. The young reindeer are skating and sledding and building snowmen. What fun it is to play in the winter snow!

Fun for all except one little reindeer. "Look at funny Rudolph!" the others cried. "His nose is bigger and redder than a tomato. And look how it shines!"

"I brought my sled to play, too," said Rudolph.

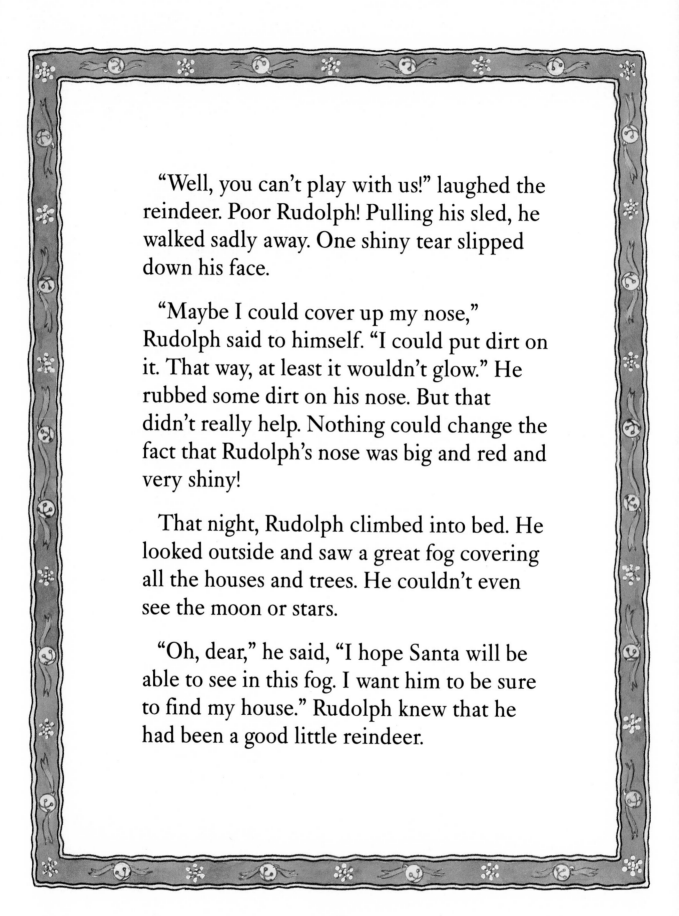

"Well, you can't play with us!" laughed the reindeer. Poor Rudolph! Pulling his sled, he walked sadly away. One shiny tear slipped down his face.

"Maybe I could cover up my nose," Rudolph said to himself. "I could put dirt on it. That way, at least it wouldn't glow." He rubbed some dirt on his nose. But that didn't really help. Nothing could change the fact that Rudolph's nose was big and red and very shiny!

That night, Rudolph climbed into bed. He looked outside and saw a great fog covering all the houses and trees. He couldn't even see the moon or stars.

"Oh, dear," he said, "I hope Santa will be able to see in this fog. I want him to be sure to find my house." Rudolph knew that he had been a good little reindeer.

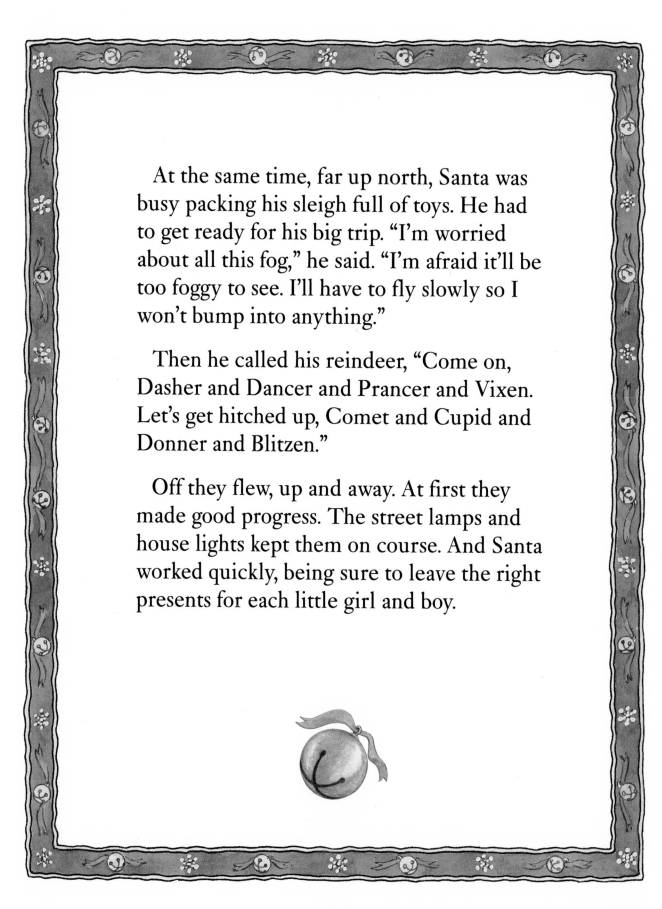

At the same time, far up north, Santa was busy packing his sleigh full of toys. He had to get ready for his big trip. "I'm worried about all this fog," he said. "I'm afraid it'll be too foggy to see. I'll have to fly slowly so I won't bump into anything."

Then he called his reindeer, "Come on, Dasher and Dancer and Prancer and Vixen. Let's get hitched up, Comet and Cupid and Donner and Blitzen."

Off they flew, up and away. At first they made good progress. The street lamps and house lights kept them on course. And Santa worked quickly, being sure to leave the right presents for each little girl and boy.

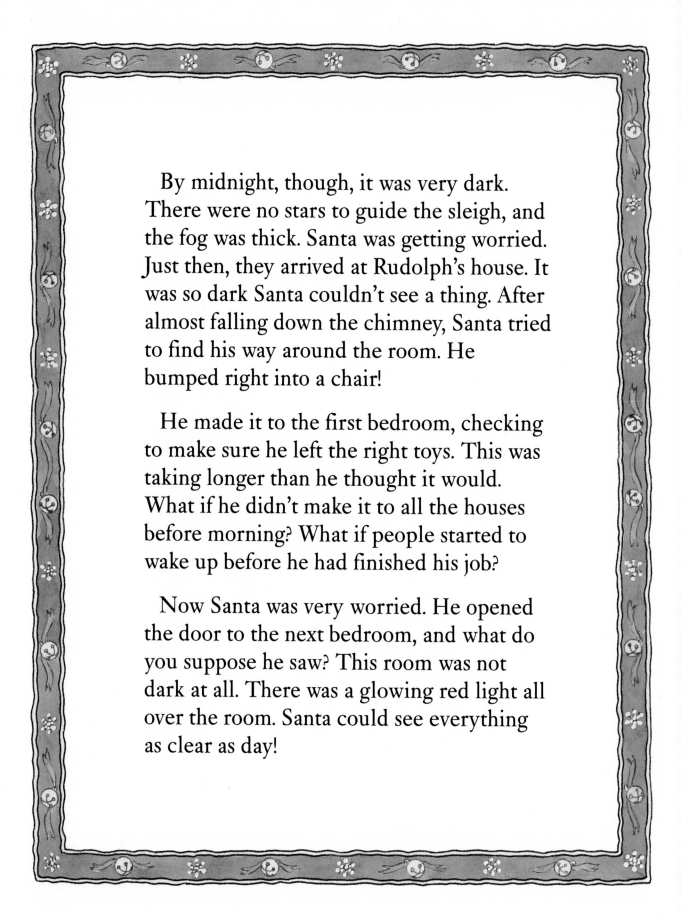

By midnight, though, it was very dark. There were no stars to guide the sleigh, and the fog was thick. Santa was getting worried. Just then, they arrived at Rudolph's house. It was so dark Santa couldn't see a thing. After almost falling down the chimney, Santa tried to find his way around the room. He bumped right into a chair!

He made it to the first bedroom, checking to make sure he left the right toys. This was taking longer than he thought it would. What if he didn't make it to all the houses before morning? What if people started to wake up before he had finished his job?

Now Santa was very worried. He opened the door to the next bedroom, and what do you suppose he saw? This room was not dark at all. There was a glowing red light all over the room. Santa could see everything as clear as day!

It wasn't a lamp that lit up the room. It wasn't the moon or the stars making it glow. No, it was Rudolph's red nose! Santa's job in this room was easy. He could see exactly which gift to leave for the little reindeer. He was happy when he went out the door.

But the rest of the house was as dark as ever. Then, suddenly, Santa had a GREAT IDEA! He went back to Rudolph's room and quickly woke him.

Rudolph couldn't believe his eyes. There, right next to his very own bed, was Santa. "Rudolph, you can help me!" said Santa.

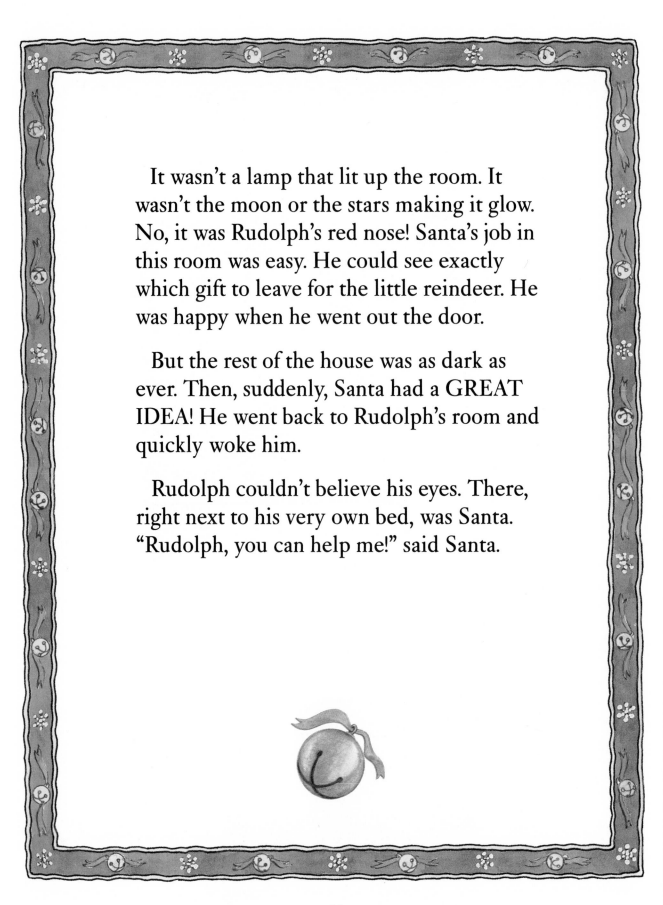

"The fog and darkness are slowing me down. I might not make it to every boy and girl's house before morning."

"But, what can I do?" asked Rudolph. Santa answered, "I need you to guide us through the fog. Your shiny nose will light the way!" That was all Rudolph needed. Of course he would help. (Wouldn't you?)

Quick as a wink, Rudolph wrote a note to his family. It said, "I've gone to help Santa. Don't worry. I'll be back by morning. Love, Rudolph." Santa dashed away to bring his sleigh down to the lawn so Rudolph could join his reindeer team.

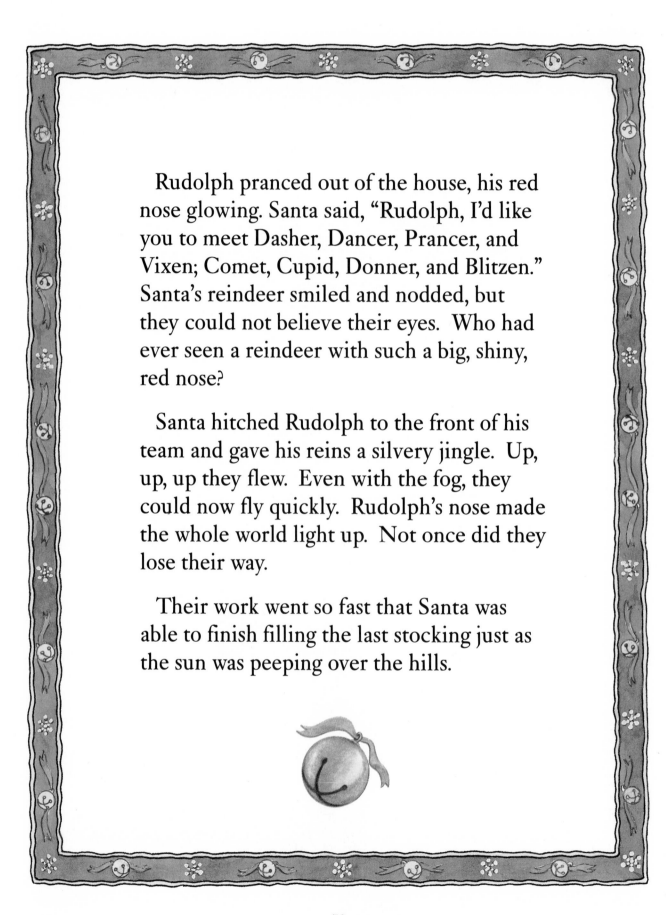

Rudolph pranced out of the house, his red nose glowing. Santa said, "Rudolph, I'd like you to meet Dasher, Dancer, Prancer, and Vixen; Comet, Cupid, Donner, and Blitzen." Santa's reindeer smiled and nodded, but they could not believe their eyes. Who had ever seen a reindeer with such a big, shiny, red nose?

Santa hitched Rudolph to the front of his team and gave his reins a silvery jingle. Up, up, up they flew. Even with the fog, they could now fly quickly. Rudolph's nose made the whole world light up. Not once did they lose their way.

Their work went so fast that Santa was able to finish filling the last stocking just as the sun was peeping over the hills.

The morning sun also woke the reindeer at Rudolph's house. Papa Reindeer was up first, and he found Rudolph's note. "What's this?" he said. "Our Rudolph has gone to help Santa Claus? Who would have ever thought such a thing." "Our Rudolph!?!" said Mama Reindeer.

Word spread quickly through the town. The reindeer gathered outside Rudolph's house to wait for his return. "You mean Rudolph, with the funny red nose, is helping Santa Claus?" they asked.

This was hard to believe. That quiet, lonely reindeer—was he really the hero of Christmas? Everyone knows that riding with Santa is the greatest honor a reindeer can have.

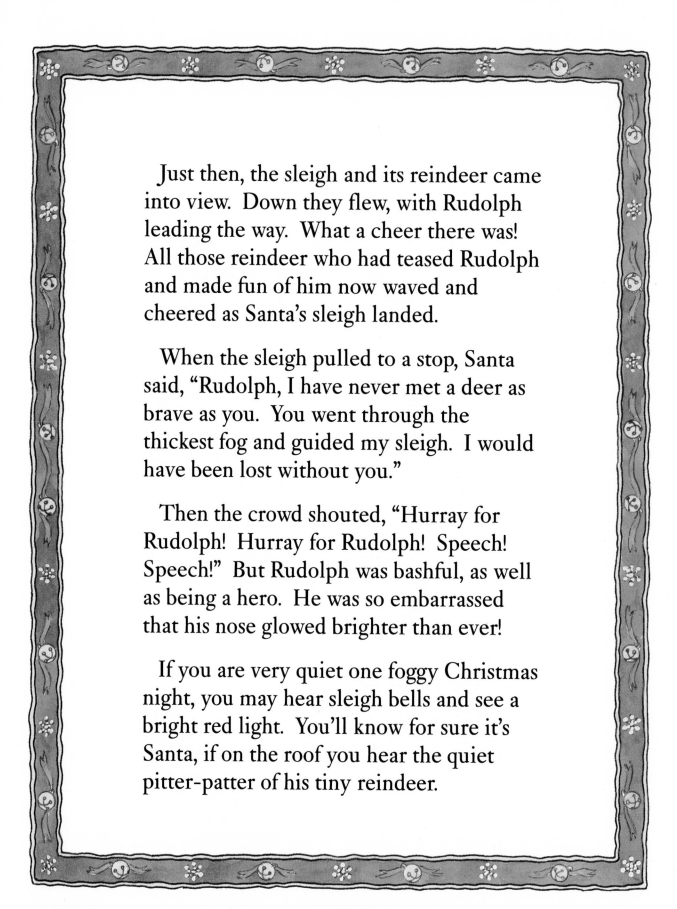

Just then, the sleigh and its reindeer came into view. Down they flew, with Rudolph leading the way. What a cheer there was! All those reindeer who had teased Rudolph and made fun of him now waved and cheered as Santa's sleigh landed.

When the sleigh pulled to a stop, Santa said, "Rudolph, I have never met a deer as brave as you. You went through the thickest fog and guided my sleigh. I would have been lost without you."

Then the crowd shouted, "Hurray for Rudolph! Hurray for Rudolph! Speech! Speech!" But Rudolph was bashful, as well as being a hero. He was so embarrassed that his nose glowed brighter than ever!

If you are very quiet one foggy Christmas night, you may hear sleigh bells and see a bright red light. You'll know for sure it's Santa, if on the roof you hear the quiet pitter-patter of his tiny reindeer.

Up at the North Pole, Santa was getting ready for his Christmas Eve trip. The weather outside was getting foggy, so Santa was in a hurry to get started.

Can you help him find these things to pack in his sleigh?

His list

His earmuffs

A thermos

A lunch box

His map

Binoculars

Reindeer fuel

A flashlight

The night was coming to an end and Santa's sleigh was approaching Reindeer Town with Rudolph in front. Rudolph wondered if anyone would believe his wonderful Christmas adventure. What do YOU believe? Did Rudolph go down in history or not?

Find our hero. Then find these things honoring Rudolph.

Rudolph

A bouquet of roses

A shiny new car

A fan letter

A key to the city

A magazine

A TV special

The newspaper

WELCOME HOME RUDY

EXTRA! RED NOSE SAVES X-MAS!

YOU'LL GO DOWN IN HISTORY

THANKS FOR CHRISTMAS RUDOLPH!

BUCK BOOKS

REVISED HISTORY BOOKS

SOLD OUT

RUDOLPH SLEPT HERE!

TIMES

EXTRA! RED NOSE SAVES XMAS!

Reindeer Magnet

MATERIALS
Poms: 1-inch beige, 2-inch brown,
  ¼-inch red
Felt: 1 x 1 inch red, 2 x 2 inches
  brown
Two wiggle eyes, 10mm each
Two beige chenille stems, 12 inches
  each
Red rattail cord, 12-inch length
Magnet strip, ¾-inch length of
  ½-inch wide
Thick white craft glue
Scissors
Ruler

1. To make the reindeer head and muzzle, glue the beige pom to the lower front part of the brown pom. For the nose, glue the red pom to the upper front part of the muzzle. Cut a smiling-mouth shape from the red felt and glue it below the nose. Glue the wiggle eyes to the head so that the bottom edges of the eyes touch the top of the muzzle.

80

Christmas List
Cookies and milk for Santa
Carrots for the reindeer
Decorate stocking
Wrap Grandma's present
Make reindeer magnet for Grandpa
Bake cookies for class party
Don't forget Amy's present
Help decorate tree

Merry Christmas

2. Measure and cut one chenille stem into a 5-inch length and a 7-inch length. Measure and cut the other chenille stem into two 6-inch lengths; you will use only one of the 6-inch lengths, so set the other one aside. To make the antlers, line up the middles of the three lengths of chenille stem. Twist the stems in the middle to join them together. Arrange the stems so the 7-inch length is on the bottom, the 6-inch length is in the middle, and the 5-inch length is on top. Pinch and curl each of the six ends up to form the antlers, as in the drawing. Glue the middle of the antlers to the back of the head.

3. Using the pattern shown, trace and cut two ears from the brown felt. Apply a dot of glue to the

bottom of one ear; pinch the bottom together and hold it for a moment. Repeat this gluing process to make the other ear. Glue the ears to the head just in front of the antlers.

4. Tie a bow in the rattail cord, then tie small knots at each end of the bow. Glue the bow beneath the muzzle. Glue the magnet strip to the back of the head.

Ear
(cut two)

CHRISTMAS RECIPES

Clockwise from top left: Snickerdoodles, Santa's Favorite Rocky Road Brownies, Layered Fudge, Holiday Sugar Cookies, Caramel-Marshmallow Apples, Mrs. Claus' Best Cookie Bars, Quick Chocolate Softies, Snowflake Pretzels, Peanut Butter Chocolate Chippers, and Old-Fashioned Popcorn Balls.

Peanut Butter Chocolate Chippers

1 cup creamy or chunky peanut butter
1 cup firmly packed light brown sugar
1 large egg
¾ cup milk chocolate chips
¼ cup granulated sugar

1. Preheat oven to 350°F. Combine peanut butter, sugar and egg in medium bowl until well blended. Add chips; mix well.

2. Roll heaping tablespoonfuls of dough into 1½-inch balls; place 2 inches apart on ungreased cookie sheet.

3. Dip fork into granulated sugar; press criss-cross pattern in each ball, flattening to ½-inch thickness.

4. Bake 12 minutes or until set. Cool for 2 minutes. Remove cookies from cookie sheet with spatula and place on wire rack; cool completely. Store in virtually airtight Tupperware® container at room temperature or freeze up to 3 months.

Makes about 2 dozen cookies

Holiday Sugar Cookies

1 cup butter or margarine, softened
¾ cup sugar
1 egg
2 cups all-purpose flour
1 teaspoon baking powder
¼ teaspoon ground cinnamon
¼ teaspoon salt
   Colored sprinkles or sugar,
      for decorating (optional)

1. Place butter and sugar in large bowl; beat with electric mixer at medium speed until creamy. Add egg; beat until fluffy. Stir in flour, baking powder, cinnamon and salt; mix until blended.

2. Shape dough into a ball; cover with plastic wrap and flatten. Place dough in refrigerator to chill until firm, about 2 hours.

3. Preheat oven to 350°F. Roll out dough, a small amount at a time, to ¼-inch thickness on lightly floured surface with lightly floured rolling pin. (Keep remaining dough in refrigerator.) Cut with 3-inch cookie cutter. Sprinkle with colored sprinkles, if desired*. Place on ungreased cookie sheet.

4. Bake 7 to 9 minutes or until edges are lightly browned. Cool on cookie sheet for 1 minute. Remove cookies from cookie sheet with spatula and place on wire rack; cool completely. Store in virtually airtight Tupperware® container at room temperature.

Makes about 3 dozen cookies

*Note: If desired, brush cookies with beaten egg white before decorating with sprinkles.

Caramel-Marshmallow Apples

1 package (14 ounces) caramels, unwrapped
1 cup mini marshmallows
2 tablespoons water
6 small apples
6 flat sticks

1. Cover baking sheet with waxed paper; spray with nonstick cooking spray.

2. Place caramels, marshmallows and water in medium saucepan. Cook over medium heat, while stirring constantly, until caramels are melted and smooth. Remove from heat and cool slightly while getting apples ready.

3. Rinse and dry apples. Insert flat sticks into stem ends of apples.

4. Dip each apple in caramel mixture, completely coating apple. Scrape apple bottom on edge of pan to remove extra caramel. Place on baking sheet. Repeat with remaining apples. Place baking sheet in refrigerator; chill until firm.

Makes 6 apples

Snickerdoodles

1½ cups sugar
1 cup butter or margarine, softened
2 eggs
2 teaspoons vanilla
2½ cups all-purpose flour
2 teaspoons cream of tartar
1 teaspoon baking soda
¼ cup sugar
1 tablespoon ground cinnamon

1. Preheat oven to 400°F. Place sugar and butter in large bowl; beat with electric mixer at medium speed until creamy. Add eggs and vanilla; beat until fluffy. Combine flour, cream of tartar and baking soda in medium bowl. Stir into butter mixture; mix well.

2. Combine sugar and cinnamon in small bowl. Shape dough into 1-inch balls. Roll balls in cinnamon-sugar mixture. Place on ungreased cookie sheet.

3. Bake 8 to 10 minutes or until set. Cool on cookie sheet for 1 minute. Remove cookies from cookie sheet with spatula and place on wire rack; cool completely. Store in virtually airtight Tupperware® container at room temperature.

Makes about 4 dozen cookies

Santa's Favorite Rocky Road Brownies

- 1 cup butter or margarine
- 4 squares (1 ounce each) unsweetened chocolate
- 1½ cups sugar
- 1 cup all-purpose flour
- 3 eggs
- 1½ teaspoons vanilla
- ½ cup salted peanuts, chopped Rocky Road Frosting (Recipe follows)

1. Preheat oven to 350°F. Place butter and chocolate in large saucepan. Cook over medium heat, while stirring constantly, until melted and smooth, about 5 to 7 minutes. Remove from heat. Stir in sugar, flour, eggs, vanilla and peanuts.

2. Spray 13 × 9-inch baking pan with nonstick cooking spray. Spread batter into pan.

3. Bake 20 to 25 minutes or until brownie starts to pull away from sides of pan. Place pan on wire rack; cool completely. While brownies are baking, make the Rocky Road Frosting.

Makes about 4 dozen brownies

Rocky Road Frosting

- ¼ cup butter or margarine
- 1 package (3 ounces) cream cheese
- 1 square (1 ounce) unsweetened chocolate
- ¼ cup milk
- 2¾ cups powdered sugar
- 1 teaspoon vanilla
- 2 cups mini marshmallows
- 1 cup salted peanuts

1. Place butter, cream cheese, chocolate and milk in medium saucepan. Cook over medium heat, while stirring constantly, until melted and smooth, about 6 to 8 minutes. Remove from heat.

2. Add powdered sugar and vanilla to chocolate mixture. Beat with electric mixer at medium speed until smooth. Stir in marshmallows and peanuts. Spread frosting over cooled brownies and cut into bars. Store in virtually airtight Tupperware® container in refrigerator.

Layered Fudge

1 cup (6 ounces) semisweet
   chocolate chips
1 can (14 ounces) sweetened
   condensed milk, divided
1 teaspoon vanilla
1 cup mini marshmallows
2 cups (12 ounces) butterscotch chips
½ cup chopped pecans

1. Spray 8-inch square pan with nonstick cooking spray.

2. Place chocolate chips in medium saucepan; cook over very low heat until chips are melted, stirring constantly. Remove from heat. Add ¾ cup of condensed milk and vanilla; stir until smooth. Stir in the marshmallows; pour mixture into pan. Place pan in refrigerator; chill until firm.

3. Place butterscotch chips in small saucepan. Cook over very low heat, while stirring constantly, until melted. Remove saucepan from heat. Add remaining condensed milk and stir until mixture is smooth. Add pecans.

4. Let butterscotch mixture cool to room temperature. Pour cooled butterscotch mixture over chilled chocolate mixture. Place pan in refrigerator; chill until firm. Remove pan from refrigerator and cut fudge into squares. Store in virtually airtight Tupperware® container in refrigerator.

Makes about 2 pounds fudge

Hint: For a different look, make butterscotch layer first and top it with the chocolate layer.

Old-Fashioned Popcorn Balls

12 cups popped popcorn
    (about ¾ cup unpopped)
1½ cups sugar
⅓ cup water
⅓ cup corn syrup
2 tablespoons butter or margarine
1 teaspoon vanilla
   Candy thermometer
   Lollipop sticks (optional)

1. Preheat oven to 250°F. Spray large, shallow roasting pan with nonstick cooking spray. Add popped popcorn and place in oven.

2. Place sugar, water and corn syrup in heavy 2-quart saucepan. Stir over low heat until sugar melts and mixture boils. Carefully clip candy thermometer to side of pan, making sure bulb does not touch bottom of pan. Cook over low heat, about 10 minutes. (If sugar crystals form on side of pan, scrape them off with a pastry brush dipped in warm water.) When thermometer reads 280°F, immediately remove pan from heat. Stir in butter and vanilla; mix until smooth.

3. Remove roasting pan from oven. Pour hot syrup mixture slowly over warm popcorn, turning pan to coat evenly. Set aside until cool but warm enough to shape. Butter hands. Working quickly, lightly press mixture into 2-inch balls. If desired, insert lollipop sticks while still warm.

4. Cool completely. Store in virtually airtight Tupperware® container at room temperature.

Makes about 14 popcorn balls

Snowflake Pretzels

8 ounces confectionery coating or
   white baking bars
1 teaspoon shortening
24 regular-size pretzel twists
   (about 3 ounces)

1. Cover baking sheet with waxed paper.

2. Place confectionery coating and shortening in small glass or metal bowl. Put small bowl in a larger bowl of hot, but not boiling, water. Stir the coating constantly until completely melted and smooth.

3. Drop pretzels into coating one at a time. Remove pretzels with a fork; let extra coating drip back into bowl. Place coated pretzels on baking sheet; let stand until coating is hard, about 30 minutes. Store in vitually airtight Tupperware® container at room temperature. *Makes 24 pretzels*

Hint: Add raisins to any leftover coating. Drop teaspoonfuls of the raisin-coating mixture onto covered baking sheet. Let raisins stand until the coating is hard, about 30 minutes.

Quick Chocolate Softies

- 1 package (18¼ ounce) devil's food chocolate cake mix
- ⅓ cup water
- ¼ cup butter or margarine, softened
- 1 large egg
- 1 cup large vanilla baking chips
- ½ cup coarsely chopped walnuts

1. Preheat oven to 350°F. Spray cookie sheet with nonstick cooking spray.

2. Place cake mix, water, butter and egg in large bowl. Beat with electric mixer at low speed until moistened. Scrape sides of bowl with a rubber spatula to remove batter. Increase speed to medium; beat 1 minute. Scrape sides of bowl with a rubber spatula to remove batter. Add chips and walnuts and stir with mixing spoon until blended.

3. Drop heaping teaspoonfuls of dough 2 inches apart (for smaller cookies) or heaping tablespoonfuls of dough 3 inches apart (for larger cookies) onto greased cookie sheet.

4. Bake 10 to 12 minutes. Cool on cookie sheet for 1 minute. Remove from sheet with spatula and place on wire rack; cool completely. Store in virtually airtight Tupperware® container at room temperature or freeze up to 3 months.

Makes about 2 dozen large or 4 dozen small cookies

Mrs. Claus' Best Cookie Bars

- 24 graham cracker squares
- 1 cup semisweet chocolate chips
- 1 cup flaked coconut
- ¾ cup coarsely chopped walnuts
- 1 can (14 ounces) sweetened condensed milk

1. Preheat oven to 350°F. Spray 13 × 9-inch baking pan with nonstick cooking spray.

2. Place graham crackers in food processor; process until crackers form fine crumbs. Measure 2 cups of crumbs. Combine graham cracker crumbs, chocolate chips, coconut and walnuts in medium bowl until blended. Add milk; stir until blended.

3. Spread batter evenly into prepared pan. Bake 15 to 18 minutes or until edges are golden brown.

4. Place pan on wire rack; cool completely. Cut into 2¼ × 2¼-inch bars. Store in vitually airtight Tupperware® container at room temperature. *Makes 20 bars*

CHRISTMAS CAROLS

Up On The Housetop

Up on the housetop reindeer pause;
    Out jumps good old Santa Claus,
Down through the chimney with lots of toys,
    All for the little ones' Christmas joys.

CHORUS:
Ho, ho, ho, who wouldn't go?
    Ho, ho, ho, who wouldn't go?
Up on the housetop, click, click, click,
    Down through the chimney with good Saint Nick.

First comes the stocking of little Nell;
    Oh, dear Santa, fill it well;
Give her a dolly that laughs and cries,
    One that can open and shut its eyes.

CHORUS

Look in the stocking of little Bill;
    Oh, just see that glorious fill!
Here is a hammer and lots of tacks,
    Whistle and ball and a set of jacks.

CHORUS

Deck The Halls

Deck the halls with boughs of holly,
    Fa la la la la la la la la.
'Tis the season to be jolly,
    Fa la la la la la la la la.
Don we now our gay apparel,
    Fa la la la la la la la la.
Troll the ancient Yuletide carol,
    Fa la la la la la la la la.

See the blazing Yule before us,
    Fa la la la la la la la la.
Strike the harp and join the chorus,
    Fa la la la la la la la la.
Follow me in merry measure,
    Fa la la la la la la la la.
While I tell of Yuletide treasure,
    Fa la la la la la la la la.

Joy To The World

Joy to the world! the Lord has come:
    Let earth receive her King.
Let ev'ry heart prepare Him room,
    And heav'n and nature sing, and heav'n and nature sing,
And heav'n and heav'n and nature sing.

Joy to the world! the Savior reigns:
    Let men their songs employ,
While fields and floods, rocks, hills, and plains,
    Repeat the sounding joy, repeat the sounding joy,
Repeat, repeat the sounding joy.

He rules the world with truth and grace,
    And makes the nations prove
The glories of His righteousness,
    And wonders of His love, and wonders of His love,
And wonders, wonders of His love.

Hark! The Herald Angels Sing

Hark! the herald angels sing,
    Glory to the newborn King!
Peace on earth and mercy mild,
    God and sinners reconciled.
Joyful, all ye nations rise,
    Join the triumph of the skies;
With the angelic host proclaim,
    Christ is born in Bethlehem.

CHORUS:
Hark, the herald angels sing,
Glory to the newborn King!

Christ by highest heav'n adored;
    Christ the everlasting Lord!
Late in time behold Him come,
    Offspring of a Virgin's womb.
Veiled in flesh the Godhead see;
    Hail the incarnate Deity.
Pleased as man with man to dwell,
    Jesus, our Emanuel!

CHORUS

Hail the heav'n born Prince of Peace!
    Hail the Son of Righteousness!
Light and life to all He brings,
    Ris'n with healing in His wings.
Mild He lays His glory by,
    Born that man no more may die.
Born to raise the sons of earth;
    Born to give them second birth.

CHORUS

We Wish You A Merry Christmas

We wish you a Merry Christmas; We wish you a Merry Christmas;
    We wish you a Merry Christmas and a Happy New Year.

CHORUS:
Good tidings to you wherever you are;
    Good tidings for Christmas and a Happy New Year.

Oh bring us a figgy pudding; Oh bring us a figgy pudding;
    Oh bring us a figgy pudding and a cup of good cheer.

CHORUS

We won't go until we've got some; We won't go until we've got some;
    We won't go until we've got some, so bring some out here.

CHORUS

We wish you a Merry Christmas; We wish you a Merry Christmas;
    We wish you a Merry Christmas and a Happy New Year.

O Christmas Tree

O Christmas tree, O Christmas tree, thy leaves are so unchanging.
O Christmas tree, O Christmas tree, thy leaves are so unchanging.

Not only green when summer's here, but also when 'tis cold and drear.
O Christmas tree, O Christmas tree, thy leaves are so unchanging.

O Christmas tree, O Christmas tree, you fill all hearts with laughter.
O Christmas tree, O Christmas tree, you fill all hearts with laughter.

On Christmas day you stand so tall, affording joy to one and all.
O Christmas tree, O Christmas tree, you fill all hearts with laughter.

Silent Night

Silent night, holy night, All is calm, all is bright.
Round yon Virgin Mother and child,
Holy Infant so tender and mild,
Sleep in heavenly peace; Sleep in heavenly peace.

Silent night, holy night, Shepherds quake at the sight.
Glories stream from heaven afar,
Heav'nly hosts sing Alleluia;
Christ the Savior is born; Christ the Savior is born.

Silent night, holy night, Son of God, love's pure light;
Radiant beams from Thy holy face,
With the dawn of redeeming grace,
Jesus, Lord at Thy birth; Jesus, Lord at Thy birth.

O Little Town Of Bethlehem

O little town of Bethlehem, how still we see thee lie;
  Above thy deep and dreamless sleep, the silent stars go by.
Yet in thy dark streets shineth the everlasting light;
  The hopes and fears of all the years are met in thee tonight.

For Christ is born of Mary, and gather'd all above,
  While mortals sleep, the angels keep their watch of wond'ring love.
O morning stars together proclaim the holy birth,
  And praises sing to God the King and peace to men on earth.

O holy Child of Bethlehem, descend to us, we pray;
  Cast out our sin and enter in; be born to us today.
We hear the Christmas angels, the great glad tidings tell;
  O come to us, abide with us, our Lord Emanuel.

Jingle Bells

Dashing through the snow,
  in a one-horse open sleigh,
O'er the fields we go,
  laughing all the way.
Bells on bobtail ring,
  making spirits bright;
What fun it is to ride and sing
  a sleighing song tonight.

Oh! jingle bells, jingle bells, jingle all the way;
  Oh, what fun it is to ride in a one-horse open sleigh. Hey!
Jingle bells, jingle bells, jingle all the way;
  Oh, what fun it is to ride in a one-horse open sleigh!

Flip back to the Look & Find™ of Santa's Workshop, where the elves are really going crazy trying to finish up all the gifts. Can you find these elves?

☐ An elf who has lost his marbles
☐ An elf who has flipped his lid
☐ An elf who is not all there
☐ An elf who has gone nuts
☐ An elf who is one brick short of a load
☐ An elf who has become cuckoo
☐ An elf who has a screw loose

Go back to the Night Before Christmas Look & Find™ where everyone is tucked in for the night—or should be. Can you find these night sights?

☐ A night "mare"
☐ A "knight" club
☐ A night owl
☐ "Knight" fall
☐ Night school
☐ Florence Nightingale
☐ A dream boat
☐ A starfish
☐ A "moon" light

Turn back to the The Happy Snowman Look & Find™ and see if you can find these funny things.

☐ A dog dressed like its master
☐ Two snow officers
☐ A singing jailbird
☐ A huntsman who's found a "fox"
☐ An invisible pet
☐ "Saw"-berry shortcake
☐ A leaky customer
☐ A boy in a sticky situation